DRAG RACING FUNNY CARS of the 1960s
PHOTO ARCHIVE
FROM SUPER STOCKERS TO FLOPPERS

Lou Hart

Iconografix
Photo Archive Series

Iconografix
PO Box 446
Hudson, Wisconsin 54016 USA

© 2003 Lou Hart

All rights reserved. No part of this work may be reproduced or used in any form by any means... graphic, electronic, or mechanical, including photocopying, recording, taping, or any other information storage and retrieval system... without written permission of the publisher.

The information in this book is true and complete to the best of our knowledge. All recommendations are made without any guarantee on the part of the author or Publisher, who also disclaim any liability incurred in connection with the use of this data or specific details.

We acknowledge that certain words, such as model names and designations, mentioned herein are the property of the trademark holder. We use them for purposes of identification only. This is not an official publication.

Iconografix books are offered at a discount when sold in quantity for promotional use. Businesses or organizations seeking details should write to the Marketing Department, Iconografix, at the above address.

Library of Congress Control Number: 2003103523

ISBN 1-58388-097-6

03 04 05 06 07 08 09 5 4 3 2 1

Printed in China

Cover and book design by Dan Perry

Copyediting by Suzie Helberg

COVER PHOTO: See page 116

BOOK PROPOSALS

Iconografix is a publishing company specializing in books for transportation enthusiasts. We publish in a number of different areas, including Automobiles, Auto Racing, Buses, Construction Equipment, Emergency Equipment, Farming Equipment, Railroads & Trucks. The Iconografix imprint is constantly growing and expanding into new subject areas.

Authors, editors, and knowledgeable enthusiasts in the field of transportation history are invited to contact the Editorial Department at Iconografix, Inc., PO Box 446, Hudson, WI 54016.

ACKNOWLEDGMENTS

I wish to thank my family and friends to whom this book would not be possible without:

• Bob Thompson and Al Nosse for their photo contributions,
• Paul Katata, for his endless supply of research materials,
• Steve and Marie Delgadillo for their contributions to this book and our thirty plus years of a great friendship,
• Jay, Karen, Rei, Michael, Ryan, and Roger at Jack's Camera for their efforts and countless hours of hard work,
• Bob and Glenda Gibson, for their desire and dedication of restoring these great funny cars from the 1960s and whose impact and background was overwhelming.
• And to my great friend Dale Kunesh - during our high school days we braved the elements of the standing room only Saturday nights at the 'Dale and the County!

Thank you to One and All!

FOREWORD
by Randy Walls

I started drag racing when I was twenty-one with a 1957 Chevy I built myself, then later with a 1960 Chevy Impala powered by a 327 c.i. engine, turning a best ever 13.04 ET running at 106 mph.

After being successful with the Impala, I sold it and built a C/MP 1955 Chevy, which turned in a national record on the first day it competed, and I improved from there. I graduated in 1965 to a supercharged 427 c.i. altered wheelbase 1965 Super Nova Chevy II, having much success racing against the likes of Richard Schroeder, "Peanut," the "Jolly Green Giant," the "Bloomin' Bullit," and "Fast" Eddie Schartman match racing at San Diego Raceway in Ramona, California.

With a new "topless" Chevy Corvair I purchased from Hayden Proffitt in 1966, I went on an eastern tour, competing at drag strips from Miami to Kansas City, with many cities in-between. I ran a big block Chevy 427 on alcohol, then quickly converted to percentages of nitromethane.

I don't think I ever feared any other racer or team, but I was always up to the challenge of racing the so called "big guns" in funny cars; the "Chi-Town Hustler", Gene Snow, Nelson Carter, "Big John" Mazmanian, and Mickey Thompson's army of funny cars.

At times, I rose to the occasion and typically won the match race or event race attended by these funny car giants. I always raced my own race regardless of who I was racing, and tried to cut a perfect light. I ran hard and I wanted to give the fans their money's worth to see good-quality racing.

In 1968 as disaster struck, the Pisano Bros. Corvair crashed into me at Irwindale Raceway, demolishing my Corvair and breaking my back and neck. Recovering from injuries was a long process, but I desired to return to getting behind the wheel to be with my peers and friends, getting more and more anxious to drive 190 mph plus!

I enjoyed my most successful season in drag racing after returning from my injuries in 1969. I won 80 percent of the approximately 70 match races and events I entered.

I won a Sixty-Four funny car field at OCIR (Orange County International Raceway) with a recorded .500-second final round reaction time on the christmas tree. At the *Popular Hot Rodding* Magazine Meet in Martin, Michigan I took runner-up honors to Fred Goeske's Hemi 'Cuda as the transmission broke.

One of my career highlights consisted of the enjoyment of the ride itself. The car performed setting track records, match races and event wins. What a thrill!

What I really liked about drag racing was the competition and camaraderie of my fellow funny car combatants. The toughest thing I found out about this type of racing was to stay technically one step ahead of the competition. If you didn't you never won! I never took losing hard, but I used losing to learn how to win and to be competitive!

I loved the smoky burnouts - the pure adrenaline rush of having 1,500 horsepower in front of and under me when I mashed down on the accelerator - it was awesome!

One of my favorite racetracks was Lions Drag Strip. It was the greatest place to race - C. J. "Pappy" Hart always treated me with respect and made me feel that I was an important part of Lions.

U.S. 30 Dragway in Gary, Indiana had a lot of great racing too! I would sometimes race two times a week during the summer months. Along with the great fans and stiff competition, there was always a lot of action.

I was very fortunate that I never had a car fire or exploded a motor. I used a totally stock Chevy crankshaft, block and heads, and I always figured I could stretch my luck a long way as long as I never detonated.

I share with you these most special times in my life, and while I enjoyed the competition, I enjoyed the people, the fans that made drag racing what it was then and what it is today!

Lou Hart Photo

INTRODUCTION

In 1959, a group of Chrysler Motor Division engineers and hot rod enthusiasts from Detroit, Michigan, known as "The Ramchargers," pooled their talents and ideas and built a highly modified 1949 Plymouth Business coupe that started the development of the funny car. The "High and Mighty," minus its rear fenders and cut up front fenders for an unusual trumpeted exhaust system, ran a Chrysler Hemi with dual four-barrel carburetors fitted on an unique intake induction system. The coupe ran in the low 12-second bracket at speeds of over 115 mph.

In 1961, the Ramchargers built another hot Super Stock Dodge with sponsorship backing from Chrysler, and thus started the manufacturer's wars between Detroit's "Big Three" that quickly spread throughout the country. New technology by Detroit's auto makers was to create an image that would pertain to the younger generation where performance over styling was in. Auto manufacturers were beginning to produce lighter compact automobiles stuffed with bigger cubic inches with higher horse-powered engines. With weight advantages, Detroit's involvement in drag racing was expanding with, "What wins on Sundays, sells on Mondays."

While dragsters were kings of the early 1960s, NHRA and AHRA soon developed new class groups for Factory Experimental and U/L cars for the independent and factory-backed racers who would be "Kings of the Block." This opened the door to drag racing pioneer Jack Chrisman, along with a group of Lincoln Mercury engineers, to build a Mercury Comet Cyclone powered by a Ford 427 Wedge motor coupled with a direct drive unit producing elapsed times of 10 seconds with speeds of 150 mph!

Funny cars were quickly developing into over night crowd pleasers! They were Detroit's iron. Early A/FXs and funny cars were steel-bodied replicas of the muscle and pony cars with lightweight acid-dipped hoods, bumpers and doors. They featured altered wheel bases with fuel-injected or supercharged large cubic inch motors belching out over 1,000 horsepower and covering the quarter mile in just over eight seconds! This was pure adrenaline! This was funny car racing!

They captivated the fans with tremendous smoky burnouts and gigantic wheel stands, and they were so unpredictable that you never knew if they would go straight or end up glancing off the guardrail!

By 1966, funny car chassis were greatly refined, being built from chromoly tubing, along with one-piece fiberglass bodies. Bodies were molded from full sized replicas but aerodynamics were starting to develop, and bodies were narrowed and lowered creating a "mini" style that produced quicker elapsed times and greater speeds. Still, the rivalries continued with the manufacturers being represented by all makes from Buicks to steel-bodied Jeeps. The popular Ford vs. Chevy, East vs. West battles would headline Saturday night match races!

Heroes were born and became idolized due to their driving talents and their showmanship. Arnie "The Farmer" Beswick, "Dandy" Dick Landy, "Dyno" Don Nicholson, "Mr. Pontiac" Jess Tyree, the "Kings of Smoke" - Farkonas, Coil and Minick's "Chi-Town Hustler," Don Schumacher, "Big John" Mazmanian, and "Jungle Jim" Liberman raced for standing-room-only crowds each and every Saturday night under the lights! Heated rivalries developed including "Big John" Mazmanian's Barracuda vs. Mickey Thompson's Mach I Mustang, which always provided the fans great side-by-side competition.

As the popularity grew with the funny cars, so did the cash purses and incentives! Drivers set their sights to run a track or national record of quick elapsed times or by producing a top speed that would earn a cash bonus, which had many drivers going "all out" to grab that brass ring! Drivers would issue the "challenge" to match race one another to see who would "blow their doors off" and be Saturday night's reigning champion!

Turnout for a 16-car funny car show would produce a "forest" of 40 or more raised fiberglass bodies throughout the pits! Many cars entering the pits on open-bed trailers would even have owners and mechanics working on the cars while they were still being towed!

Orange County International Raceway in East Irvine, California hosted the annual Manufacturer's Sixty-Four Funny Car Championships where all funny cars were positioned on the track with the bodies raised up. Promoters gave the "fire up" sign and all 64 blown motors came to life at the same time, with an estimated 96,000 horsepower. An awesome sight to see and hear!

Several funny car drivers gained reputations by raising the fans to their feet! In 1968, the Chi-Town Hustler's Farkonas, Coil and Minick were approached by the track promoter at the 1/8-mile track at Drag City, in Springfield, Illinois. The promoter informed them that the track was in such poor traction condition that it was decided to extend their burnout to put heat into the tires. Driver Pat Minick laid down an incredible 1/8-mile smoky burnout and the crowd went wild! The next day at the Rockford, Illinois' 1/4-mile strip, Minick duplicated the 600-foot burnout and again the crowd went crazy, and so the Chi-Town legacy was born!

The sixties were an era of funny car successes and failures. While many were racing for Saturday night bragging rights, many raced for a living. Drivers earned the respect of their peers. Today, several of these legends made contributions to this book. I would like to thank Austin Coil, Ray Alley, Don "The Shoe" Schumacher, Linda Vaughn, Rich Siroonian, "Colonel" John Hogan, Jess Tyree, Paula Murphy, photographer Bill Crites, and especially Randy Walls. Without their help this book would not be possible. Also, to you, the fan, I dedicate this pictorial of the greatest era of funny car racing! We lived and breathed those fabulous floppers on Saturday nights, under the lights! Be there!

Located off Interstate-5 in East Irvine, California, Orange County International Raceway was the crown jewel of the West Coast. The Sixty-Four Funny Car Manufacturers Meet, PDA, All-Pro, Hang Ten Funny Car 500 Meets were some of the counties' most prestigious events. The likes of Don Schumacher, "Big John" Mazmanian, Jungle Jim, Chi-Town Hustler, and others set national records and established the careers of the modern day drag racing superstars. *Lou Hart*

In 1960, a group of Chrysler engineers and hotrod enthusiasts started the Ramchargers club and created this extremely modified 1949 Plymouth Business coupe, named the "High & Mighty." The Plymouth was powered by a Chrysler Hemi with an unusual high rise intake manifold paired with dual carburetors. The exhaust system was a unique matched set with trumpeted headers exiting from the modified front fenders. The induction scoop was raised about a foot above the roofline of the coupe. Shown here at 1960 NHRA Detroit Nationals in the C/A class, the Plymouth blazed the trail of what funny cars were to become. *Al Nosse*

The "High & Mighty" Plymouth (background) squared off against a B/A coupe at the 1960 Detroit Nationals. Note both induction systems of both coupes. The "High & Mighty" ran speeds over 115 mph with elapsed times in the 12-second range. *Al Nosse*

Another unusual B/A was Modifications Unlimited from Lexington, Maryland. The wheelbase was stretched with the engine moved forward. The roofline swooped down to provide more aerodynamics but the driver had limited vision to see down the strip. *Al Nosse*

Another example of the development of funny cars. In 1962, this fuel Ford coupe of Mooneyham & Sharp used a 114-inch wheelbase chassis with the engine set back approximately 25 percent. The coupe ran speeds around 160 mph with this setup. *Lou Hart*

Another view of the Mooneyham & Sharp 1934 Ford with the front clip removed. The motor is set back 25 percent to offset the 114-inch wheelbase. This weight distribution helped generate speeds of 160 mph. *Lou Hart*

In 1963, the Mopar Wedge engine had developed into a true high performance-equipped "Super Stock" engine, featuring dual Carter AFB carburetors bolted to a cross-ram intake manifold, tuned header system, and lightweight aluminum fenders, hood and bumpers. In a third of a series, the "Melrose Missile" S/S Plymouth was driven by Tommy Grove and Charlie Di Bari, and was sponsored by Melrose Motors of Oakland. It's shown here with Tommy Grove at the *Hot Rod* Magazine Nationals at Riverside Raceway. The "Melrose Missile" won the 1963 NHRA Winter Nationals Super Stock class with 12.00 ETs and speeds of 118 mph. *Bob Thompson*

Bill "Maverick" Golden's Dodge Coronet S/SA, shown here at the *Hot Rod* Magazine Nationals at Riverside Raceway. Powered by a 426 c.i. Max Wedge engine, the Dodge, sponsored by the Orange County Dodge Dealers, ran mid 12-second ETs with speeds above 115 mph. *Bob Thompson*

Dick Landy's Automotive Research Super Stock Dodge Coronet, sponsored by the L. A. County Dodge Dealers Association, featured a Dodge "Ramcharger" Max Wedge engine with dual carbs and a cross-ram intake manifold with Doug's Headers. *Bob Thompson*

Plymouth dealer McCullough & Ricci, Inc., of Detroit, Michigan, sponsored the "Lawman" Super Stock Plymouth driven by Al Eckstrand. A 426 Chrysler engine powered the potent Mopar to track records throughout the Midwest. *Bob Thompson*

Les Ritchey's "Performance Associates" A/FX Ford Mustang was a strong contender in the A/FX wars. The potent Mustang, shown here at Irwindale's staging lanes, ran against the likes of Arnie Beswick, Gas Ronda, "Fast" Eddie Schartman, and other factory U/L and A/FXers. *Bob Gibson*

Arnie "The Farmer" Beswick's 1963 "Tameless Tiger" at Irwindale Raceway's staging lanes. Powered by a 421 SD blown Pontiac motor, Gay Pontiac of Dickinson, Texas sponsored the popular "Poncho." Arnie Behling later crashed the Tempest. It was eventually found in a ravine. The car is restored today. *Bob Gibson*

Al VanDerWoude's "Flying Dutchman" 1964 fuel-injected 426 Dodge featured an Art Carr Torqueflite transmission with the rear axle moved to underneath the rear seat, which caused the "funny" effect. *Bob Gibson*

The Doug's Headers Chevy II Nova, driven by Doug Thorley, launches at Lions Drag Strip. Powered by a fuel-injected 427 c.i. Chevy motor, Doug was also owner and manufacturer of headers and exhaust systems for many of the A/FX funnies. *Photo courtesy of the scrapbook of Lou Hart*

Hayden Proffitt's injected Chevy Corvair blasts down the Lions quarter mile. Mickey Thompson equipment, Jardine headers and Crane cams allowed the injected 427 c.i. Chevy respectable performances. Later, Hayden would cut off the roof of the Corvair. *Photo courtesy of the scrapbook of Lou Hart*

Butch Leal's factory A/FX 1965 altered Plymouth had a 426 fuel-injected Hemi that gave the factory Ford Mustangs all they could handle. Lightweight aluminum bumpers and body panels, along with altered wheelbases, and engines moved back approximately 25 percent, gave these A/FXers their "funny" look. *Bob Gibson*

The 1965 Ford Mustang of Dick Brannan featured an injected 427 c.i. "Cammer" Ford engine sponsored by Bob Ford of Dearborn, Michigan. The factory-backed Ford Mustang reigned terror among the Chevy Novas and Pontiac Tempests. *Bob Gibson*

Charlie Wilson's "Vicious 'Vette" was shoed by Clyde Morgan, shown here at Lions Drag Strip. The 'Vette had a blown Chevy stuffed into the chassis with Jardine headers that provided the breathing for 9.30 ETs and speeds over 155 mph. *Lou Hart*

Gene Snow's "Rambunctious" started out as a wrecked 1965 Dodge Dart. Powered by a fuel-injected Chrysler 426 Hemi, Gene utilized the push button gear shifter mounted on the driver's side window post using his left elbow to shift gears and his right hand on the steering wheel. Gene ran in the B/A class at national events dominating with 8.60 ETs and 150-mph speeds. *Photo courtesy of the scrapbook of Lou Hart*

Dick Harrell's 1966 Chevy Nova, from Nickey Chevrolet of Chicago, had an injected 427 c.i. Chevy motor. Bill Thomas of Anaheim, California built the potent Nova to 9.00-second ETs -150 mph. *Bob Gibson*

Blair's Speed Shop of Pasadena, California sponsored the blown 396 c.i. Chevy II Nova of Steve Bovan. The popular Bovan later went on to drive the Imperial Customs Charger and returned to pilot the series of Blair's funny cars. *Bob Gibson*

Tom McEwen drove the Plymouth Dealers Association's "Hemi 'Cuda." The mid-engined 426 c.i. hemi was built by Dave Zeuschel Racing Engines with a TorqueMaster transmission, Mickey Thompson tires, with rods, pistons and headers by Exhaust Engineering. The 'Cuda eventually flew into the lights at Lions Drag Strip and suffered considerable damage. *Bob Gibson*

Gas Ronda's 1966 Ford Mustang was the West Coast's premier factory funny car built by Holman-Moody. A 427 SOHC fuel-injected engine powered the 2,400-pound Russ Davis Ford running respectable 8.20 ETs with speeds in excess of 160 mph. *Bob Gibson*

"Dyno" Don Nicholson's "Eliminator I" Mercury Comet set the standards by winning the 1967 AHRA and NHRA Winternationals in the unlimited and S/XS classes. The unblown 427 c.i. SOHC Ford Logghe-built Comet ran 8.20 ETs and 170-mph speeds. *Bob Gibson*

Roger Lindamood's "Color Me Gone" 1967 Dodge Charger, sponsored by Snavely & Langford Dodge of Compton, California, shown at Irwindale Raceway's East vs. West Funny Car Championships. Crewmembers franticly swap out a damaged cylinder head on the 426 Chrysler fuel-injected Hemi, which recorded an 8.20 ET with a speed of 175 mph. *Dale Kunesh*

"The flying school teacher" Kelly Chadwick drove the Steakley Bros. Chevy Town 1968 steel body Camaro prepped by Don Hardy. Powered by a blown 427 c.i. Chevy motor, Kelly set several Midwest track records running 8.50 ETs with speeds of 165 mph. *Dale Kunesh*

Simple open-bed trailers transported funny cars from race to race, like this fine example of Kenz & Leslie's "High Country Cougar" of Denver, Colorado. Kumpf Motors sponsored the blown 427 c.i. SOHC Logghe-built Mercury with Ron Leslie performing the driving chores. *Dale Kunesh*

Brothers Joe & Frank Pisano competed this 1967 blown 427 c.i. Chevy-powered Camaro shown here at Lions Drag Strip. The Camaro blazed the 1/4-mile with an 8.34 ET at 175 mph. Frankie drove the popular flip-front clipped Camaro with a unique "clamshell" hood. *Steve Delgadillo*

The "Hairy Canary" Plymouth Valiant of Hammons & Williamson from Northern California. Rich Hammons piloted the Engle-cammed 392 c.i. Chrysler Hemi Valiant Signet at Lions Drag Strip with a 9.06 ET at 173 mph. *Steve Delgadillo*

Gas Ronda's 1968 Ford Mustang built by Holman & Moody Race Cars featured an injected Ford 427 c.i. SOHC engine. Ronda, a former dance instructor, pilots his Russ Davis Ford entry at Lions Drag Strip. *Steve Delgadillo*

Jack Head Chevrolet's 1968 "Mako Shark" Corvette had a blown 427 c.i. Chevy and a factory-built Corvette body that was prepped and painted by Sperry. Roger Wolford drove the "Shark" owned by Jim Wetton and Don Cullinan. *Dale Kunesh*

J & J Enterprise's "Limefire" Barracuda from Felton, California cost more than $20,000 and took four months to build. "Limefire" was powered by a 1958 392 c.i. Chrysler Hemi bored to 400 c.i. with an Engine Masters Torqueflite transmission. Fiberglass LTD supplied the 1967 Barracuda and it was painted "Limefire" lacquer by Jim St. Clare, and driven by Claire Sanders. *Steve Delgadillo*

35

Lew Arrington's "Brutus" Pontiac Firebird featuring a Logghe-built chassis powered by an early 392 c.i. Chrysler Hemi launches here at Lions Drag Strip. Larry Hopkins Pontiac of Sunnyvale, California and San Jose's Goodies Speed Shop sponsored the popular Firebird. *Steve Delgadillo*

"Dyno" Don Nicholson's "Eliminator II" Mercury Comet dominated the competition with Earl Wade tuning the supercharged 427 c.i. SOHC Ford "Cammer" engine. With a Logghe-built tubular chassis, Don was one of the first owners/drivers to have a one-piece fiberglass bodied funny car with a tube frame chassis. *Dale Kunesh*

The chassis of "Dyno" Don Nicholson's "Eliminator II," built by Logghe Stamping Company, shows the offset roll cage, coil-over shocks, the 427 c.i. SOHC supercharged motor and fuel and dry sump oil tanks. *Dale Kunesh*

Tom Sherlock Ford sponsored "Psycho," a Ford Mustang that was actually a blown fuel altered, belonging to Ralph Snoddgrass and Pat Mahken. The bright yellow 'Stang was a local favorite in the Southern California area. It featured a 427 c.i. Ford "Wedge" motor. Larry Barkin handled the driving chores here at Lions Drag Strip in Long Beach, California. *Steve Delgadillo*

The red, white and blue Mercury Comet of Dee Keaton was another potent Comet with a Fletcher-built chassis and SOHC "Cammer" supercharged motor. Art Carr Transmission hooked the power to the 9-inch Ford rear end, and Tyree "weedburner" headers provided breathing to the 1,300-horsepower power plant running 8.50 ETs. *Steve Delgadillo*

The ex-Hayden Proffitt "topless" Chevy Corvair was owned and driven by Randy Walls. It was powered by a blown 427 c.i. Chevy engine. Randy, from San Diego, was another local favorite in the Southern California area, along with his wife Cheri. Art Carr, Chenowth Headers, and Taco Bell sponsored the wild Corvair. *Photo courtesy of Randy Walls' scrapbook*

Charlie Allen's silver and blue 1968 Dodge Dart had an M&S Welding chassis and Keith Black Chrysler Hemi power. Crenshaw Dodge sponsored the "All American Boy" from Glendora, California. *Steve Delgadillo*

Paul Candies and Leonard Hughes' beautiful candy red Plymouth Barracuda from Louisiana was one of the South's potent funny car teams. The Cajun 'Cuda featured Keith Black Hemi power, Logghe Stamping Company chassis, M&H Dragmaster slicks, and was painted by Tonti. The Barracuda body was equipped with an escape hatch, which was an uncommon feature. The bodies were latched from the outside, and if the driver encountered any problems, they had difficulty exiting the car. *Dale Kunesh*

"Fast" Eddie Schartman's "Air Lift Rattler" 1968 Mercury Cougar was another factory-backed funny car. A 427 SOHC "Cammer" motor was prepped and tuned by Arnie Behling. The Cougar featured a Logghe-built chassis, B&M transmission, Milodon engine components, Halibrand wheels, and Jardine headers. Painted pearl yellow, MPC made this a favorite model kit among fans. *Dale Kunesh*

Doug Thorley's second generation Chevy Corvair was campaigned by Dick Bourgeois and Earl Wade. The Corvair's Logghe-built chassis cradled a 427 c.i. blown Chevy tuned by Wade. Fiberglass Trends supplied the body and Watson sprayed the psychedelic paisley paint. *Dale Kunesh*

"Rapid" Ronnie Runyan boils the hides in route to an 8.25 ET at Irwindale Raceway's Third Annual Funny Car Championships. The "Blue Hell" Corvair was powered by a supercharged 427 c.i. Howard-equipped motor. A Fiberglass Trends body was matched with a Fletcher-built chassis. *Lou Hart*

Lee Jones piloted the Pontiac Firebird sponsored by A. McFadden Pontiac of Los Angeles. Fletcher Racecars of Bellflower built the Firebird. Malcolm Durham Race Engines supplied the power to run 8.40 ETs at Irwindale Raceway's New Year's Day Funny Car Championships. *Lou Hart*

Bourgeois & Wade's Corvair sponsored by Doug's Headers at Irwindale Raceway's New Year's Day Third Annual Funny Car Championships. The Chevy-powered Corvair, tuned by Earl Wade, was a strong threat in the funny car ranks throughout Southern California. Doug also fielded a rear-engined AMC Javelin funny car driven by Norm Weekly. *Lou Hart*

Sunnyvale, California's Claire Sanders drove "Jungle Jim" Liberman's number two Chevy Nova. The Logghe Bros. built the chassis and Steve Kanuika Speed Shop built the 427 c.i. blown Chevy rat motor. Claire is shown here at Irwindale Raceway during an 8.13 ET qualifying pass. Claire went on to defeat Ray Alley in the finals of the NHRA Winternational to become the first funny car champion at a national event. *Lou Hart*

The "New Breed" Pontiac Firebird steel bodied funny car featured a Fiberglass Trends flip up front clip, an M/T equipped, Steve Montrelli prepped 392 c.i. Chrysler Hemi, and a Fletcher chassis. Pete's Chevron sponsored the Firebird with "Doc" Leroy Hales handling the driving chores. *Lou Hart*

Memorable Moments of the 1960s
Nelson Carter, owner of the "Super Chief":

"In 1967 at the U.S. Nationals at Indy, I met Keith Black. I was 22 and I approached Mr. Black. I asked him about building a motor for my new funny car. I remember Keith telling me, "Speed costs money boy, how fast do you want to go?" "200 miles per hour Mr. Black!" "Well, you can call me Keith." "You can call me Nelson."

Oklahoman Nelson Carter's "Super Chief" Dodge Charger was driven by Dave Beebe. It was powered by a Keith Black 426 c.i. blown Hemi, featured a Logghe-built chassis, and was painted by Imperial Customs. Beebe ran the "Super Chief" to 7.60 ETs with speeds over 190 mph. *Lou Hart photos*

Ex-Super 'Cuda driver Larry Reyes owned and drove this beautiful Plymouth Barracuda built by Don Hardy Racecars. Coleman-Taylor Transmissions and a Keith Black Hemi made up the driveline. Larry would later opt to drive Roland Leong's "Hawaiian." *Steve Delgadillo*

Lew "Fireball" Arrington's New "Brutus II" 1968 Pontiac Firebird featured a Logghe-built chassis, a Steve Kanuika/Goodies Speed Shop-built 392 early Chrysler Hemi. Lew, from San Jose, California, waits to qualify at Irwindale Raceway. *Lou Hart*

"Mr. Pontiac," Jess Tyree, selected Mike Leiby Race Cars for the rectangular chassis, a Canadian Pontiac 440 c.i. motor, Enderle injection and a 3.90 Pontiac rear end. Dee Keaton worked the aluminum panels in the Antique Fiberglass Firebird body, which was painted by Molly of La Habra, California. Jess, running the Coca-Cola Cavalcade of Stars, ran constant 7.40 ETs with speeds of 190 mph. *Lou Hart*

Charlie Allen's 1969 Dodge Dart featured an M&S chassis with Jeff Crowther tuning the 426 Keith Black Hemi elephant. Sponsored by Saddleback Dodge, "The All-American Boy" won the 1969 *Hot Rod* Magazine Nationals at Riverside Raceway, defeating Pat Foster in Mickey Thompson's Mach I. Charlie ran a 7.59 ET with a top speed in excess of 194 mph. *Dale Kunesh*

Roland Leong's debut in the funny car wars at The NHRA Winternationals was more than he expected! Larry Reyes, driving the Logghe-built, Keith Black powered full-bodied Dodge Charger "Hawaiian" against Larry Christopherson's Chevy Nova, went airborne in the lights and violently flipped, destroying the Charger. *Dale Kunesh*

Rich Siroonian oversees the installation of "weedburner" headers on "Big John" Mazmanian's brand new 1969 Plymouth Barracuda at Doug Thorley Headers of Los Angeles. The 'Cuda debuted at Irwindale Raceway September 4, 1968, match racing against Charlie Allen's Dodge Dart. *Steve Delgadillo*

The "office" of Rich Siroonian in Big John's 'Cuda features all the comforts of a 200-mph pass down the 1/4 mile. Aluminum seat, Simpson lap and shoulder belts, Trans shifter and Grant steering wheel provided Rich a busy day at the "office." *Steve Delgadillo*

"Big John" Mazmanian's 1969 Barracuda featured an Exhibition Engineering-built chassis, Keith Black 392 c.i. Hemi tuned by Doug "Cookie" Cook, B&M transmission, and Fiberglass Trends fiberglass body. *Steve Delgadillo*

Tommy Grove launches at Irwindale Raceway with his Logghe-prepared "Going Thing" Mach I Mustang. Grove, from Northern California, was always a strong threat in match racing, winning over 60 percent of his races. *Lou Hart*

Northern California's Tommy Grove's "Going Thing" 1969 Ford Mustang featured a Logghe-built chassis cradling a SOHC 427 c.i. supercharged 1,500-horsepower engine. In 1969, Tommy gained notoriety by unofficially making the first 200-mph pass in a funny car. *Steve Delgadillo*

"Big" Eddie Lenarth's "Holy Toledo" aluminum-bodied Jeep roadster was built by Dick Fletcher Race Cars of Bellflower, California. The "yellow brick" featured a 392 Chrysler Hemi with a two-speed drive or, at times, a high gear drive only. Sponsored by Brian Chuchua's Jeep dealership, Ed ran a career best 7.52 ET at 173.74 mph, defeating Bob Smith in Sturm & Fisher's Chevy Corvair in September 1969 at OCIR. *Steve Delgadillo*

The return of Roland Leong's "Hawaiian" had a Black elephant wrapped in a Logghe chassis. Ron Scrima reworked the Fiberglass Limited mini-Charger body of Chicago. Larry Reyes remained behind the wheel with the assistance of the "Armenian Army" of "Big John" Mazmanian, Doug "Cookie" Cook, and Stan Shiroma. The "Hawaiian" swept the first three events it entered. *Lou Hart*

Gary Crane's "Travelin' Javelin" had a 392 Chrysler Hemi, Doug's Headers, and the driving talents of Dale Armstrong. Armstrong ran a strong 7.85 ET at 179 mph at Lions Drag Strip Anniversary Race. *Steve Delgadillo*

Randy Walls "lights the hides" at Lions Drag Strip. Bill Thomas Race Cars sponsored the "Super Nova II" powered by a 427 c.i. rat motor and Valley Head Service heads. Byron Racing Products of Chula Vista reworked the 6.71 supercharger. The Nova ran its best performance of 7.32ET at 206 mph. Known for his hard work and competitiveness, Randy, along with his beautiful wife Cheri, were crowd favorites. *Photo courtesy of Randy Walls' scrapbook*

This full-bodied 1969 Dodge Charger of Dallas Ferguson and Dean Hoffheins of Salt Lake City, was one of the most immaculate funny cars ever built. The "Dodge Fever" Charger, driven by Dave Beebe, sported a Logghe Brothers chassis, Keith Black 426 elephant power, Engine Masters transmission, and paint by Robles Custom of SLC. Beebe piloted the mighty Dodge to 7.60 ETs with speeds in excess of 197 mph. *Lou Hart*

Gas Ronda of Russ Davis Ford of Covina, California, pops the chute during a 7.40 ET 202.45-mph pass at the lights at Irwindale Raceway. Ronda's Mach I Mustang featured a Logghe Stamping Company chassis. Ed Pink Racing Engines of Van Nuys, California built the 1,600-horsepower SOHC "Cammer," with Skip Burroughs tuning the popular orange 'Stang. *Lou Hart*

Bob Veselka of Corpus Christi, Texas owned and drove his "Stampede" Mustang, built by Chapman Automotive Race Cars and Engines, using 4130-alloy chromoly steel tubing. Powered by a Ford 427 c.i. SOHC power plant, Bob recorded 7.30 ETs and speeds above 202 mph. *Lou Hart*

Gary "The Chicago Kid" Dyer won the 1969 Coca-Cola Cavalcade of Stars Championship driving Norm Kraus' Grand Spaulding Dodge Charger. "Mr. Norm's" mini-Charger sported a Logghe-built chassis, a Ramchargers 426 c.i. Chrysler Hemi, and the supercharger prepped by Dyer himself. "The Chicago Kid" ran constant 7.40 ETs and speeds above 200 mph. *Lou Hart*

Memorable Moment of the 1960s
Paula Murphy:
"Needing to obtain a funny car license, I needed to complete the required full pass down the quarter mile. At Lions Drag Strip in Long Beach, California, I passed and received my funny car driver's license. Needing two signatures of licensed drivers, Don Garlits and Tom McEwen signed their names to the license to certify me."

One of only five licensed women funny car pilots, Paula Murphy owned and drove the ex-Larry Reyes Plymouth Barracuda. Sid Waterman powered the Don Hardy-built 'Cuda. Paula gained notoriety at the 1969 AHRA World Championships where she clocked an incredible 7.55 ET and a 200-mph blast before bowing out to mechanical difficulties in the semi round. *Lou Hart*

Northbridge, New York's Jim Maybeck's "Screaming Eagle" Corvair featured a Rollie Lindblad-built chassis and a supercharged 427 Chevy rat motor producing an 8.04 ET at 180 mph at Irwindale Raceway. The Corvair incorporated a unique intake system; when the body was raised, the air scoop was attached to the body tin. *Lou Hart*

One of most feared and dominating funny cars in drag racing history, Mickey Thompson's Mach I, driven by Danny Ongais, set numerous national records in 1969. Powered by a Ford SOHC 427 Amos Saterlee-Stump Davis-tuned motor, Danny won the Bakersfield March Meet, Sears Point, the spring OCIR Manufacturers Sixty-Four Funny Car championships, NHRA and AHRA Spring Nationals, and NHRA U.S. Nationals. And, on September 14, 1969, he made history by being the first funny car driver to record an unofficial 6.95 ET at Kansas City International Raceway and was named Drag News Funny Car Driver of the Year. *Lou Hart*

Memorable Moment of the 1960s
Don Schumacher, owner and driver of the "Stardust" Barracuda:

"In 1968, at Orange County International Raceway with John Hogan, we had all sorts of transmission problems. Track management did not ask us to return. Curing the transmission woes, we returned the next week, raced unpaid, and set the track record with an elapsed time of 7.38."

Memorable Moment of the 1960s
John Hogan, mechanic for Don Schumacher's "Stardust" 'Cuda:

"In 1968, Don and I were at the OCIR Manufacturers Meet, our first time together there. We faced Rich Siroonian in "Big John" Mazmanian's 'Cuda in the final round and were runners-up and that started an East-West rivalry between the both of us."

Don Schumacher's "Stardust" Barracuda won the 1969 NHRA Summernationals running a 7.22 ET at 207 mph over Roland Leong's "Hawaiian." Ed Pink's Hemi elephant was prepped and tuned by John Hogan with a Logghe-built chassis. *Lou Hart*

The "Assassination Too!" Corvair of Guzman & Ward from Denver, Colorado was built by Exhibition Engineering, with a blown 427 c.i. Chevy big block and a Fiberglass Trends Corvair body. Chuck Viner Chevrolet of Denver sponsored the "mile high" Corvair. The Corvair was eventually cut up in the mid-80s and the chassis ended up in a landfill. *Dale Kunesh*

The brother and sister team of Bernie & Della Woods' 1968 Dodge Charger tipped the scales at a whopping 2,400 pounds! A blown Chrysler Hemi, tuned by Bernie, produced 7.50 ETs with speeds of 180 mph. Della, one of four licensed female funny car pilots, was the first female driver to enter an NHRA funny car national event. *Dale Kunesh*

Hank Clark pilots the Chapman Automotive "Outa' Site Too!" through the traps at Bakersfield running a 7.62 ET-196 mph. *Bob Thompson*

Chapman Automotive Race Cars and Engines' Hank Clark waits patiently to qualify in the "Outa' Site Too!" Camaro. Pat Johnson tuned the 392 Chrysler Hemi built by Chapman Automotive Race Cars and Engines. *Bob Thompson*

Chuck Hoffman drove the "Precisioned Speed Shop's" (of Buena Park, California) Chevy Corvair at Lions Drag Strip. The all steel-bodied Chevy Corvair was powered by an injected 427 c.i. rat motor and featured a squared-tube chassis. Note Chuck's plastic bubble-styled face guard, which was later banned when another injected funny car exploded, its motor causing the shield to melt to the driver's face. *Bob Thompson*

Rich Siroonian burns out "Big" John Mazmanian's 1969 Plymouth Barracuda at Irwindale Raceway. The beautiful candy red Plymouth relied on a 392 Keith Black Hemi, Doug's Headers, B&M transmission, and M&H Racemaster slicks and tires. *Lou Hart*

The Justice Brothers' "Superbird" Pontiac Firebird of "Flash" Gordon Mineo used a Howard-equipped 427 c.i. Chevrolet rat motor with Jardine headers. On one occasion, Mineo qualified the "bodiless bird" into a top fuel show, after a violent explosion destroyed the fiberglass body. *Lou Hart*

Ken Coleman's Destroyer Jeep was once campaigned by Gene Conway. Coleman's blue roadster had an early 392 c.i. Chrysler Hemi. Eventually, NHRA banned all Jeep-bodied funny cars due to weight advantages, but the Jeeps were never a serious threat to the funny car class. *Steve Delgadillo*

A Keith Black 426 Hemi inside Charlie Allen's Dodge Dart has been bored out to 440 cubic inches. Mickey Thompson pistons, Crower camshaft, and Enderle injection produced 1,500 horsepower at a cost of approximately $6,000. *Steve Delgadillo*

Twilight at Irwindale Raceway has "The Invader" Corvette driven by "Mighty" Mike Van Sant squaring off against Bob Smith in Tom Sturm's "4 Chevy Lovers" Corvair. Both floppers were constant competitors on the West Coast. *Steve Delgadillo*

"Big John" Mazmanian pulls up his pants as nephew Rich Siroonian heats up the M&H Racemaster slicks. Mazmanian, known for his dominance in the gasser wars, also became a funny car legend with his candy apple red Plymouth Barracudas. *Lou Hart*

Ray Alley's Engine Masters Plymouth Barracuda featured an early Chrysler Hemi, Engine Master transmission, and both Don Long and Ray himself constructed the chassis. Ray was runner-up to Claire Sanders at the 1969 NHRA Winternationals in Pomona, California. *Dale Kunesh*

Memorable Moment of the 1960s
Ray Alley:

"Winning the AHRA Nationals with a small block 354 c.i. Chrysler Hemi in Bristol."

81

The First Lady of drag racing, Miss Hurst, Linda Vaughn, reigned over every National drag racing event. Representing the Hurst Corporation, drag racing's ambassador was inspirational to the racers and fans alike. *Bob Thompson*

Memorable Moment of the 1960s
Linda Vaughn:

"The 1966 NHRA Winternationals at Pomona, California was my first time on the shifter platform of a convertible. Being from Georgia, I was very nervous and nearly in tears to see if I would be accepted by the California fans. In the land of movie stars, everyone overwhelmed me and I was treated like the race queen. I would also like to specially thank George Hurst and Wally Parks for everything they've done for me."

Coca-Cola Cavalcade's touring stars included high school teacher Kelly Chadwick from Texas. Chadwick's 1969 Chevy Camaro was built by Don Hardy Race Cars. A potent blown 427 c.i. Chevy rat motor powered the Steakley Brothers' Chevrolet. The "Professor" was successful in winning several Coca-Cola Cavalcade Meets setting low ETs and top speeds. *Dale Kunesh*

Another successful funny car of "Dyno" Don Nicholson was this factory-backed 1968 Mercury Cougar "Eliminator II." A Logghe-built chassis featured a 427 c.i. SOHC "Cammer" engine prepped and tuned by Pete Williams. Frank Oglesby shoed the Coca-Cola Cougar at the 1969 Winternationals. *Dale Kunesh*

Dick Bourgeois in Doug Thorley's "Javelin 2" squares off against Rusty Dellings in Marv Eldridge's Fiberglass Trends Javelin. The two funnies were the most dominant of the AMC-bodied funny cars in competition on the West Coast. Bourgeois' Javelin, along with Eldridge's AMC, together ran the Coca-Cola Cavalcade of Stars circuit throughout the country. *Steve Delgadillo*

Jess Tyree completes his burnout at Irwindale Raceway's Grand Prix. Powered by a blown Canadian Pontiac motor, Jess' Firebird ran a 7.89 ET at 188.66 mph and was a main fixture on the Coca-Cola Cavalcade of Stars circuit. *Lou Hart*

Memorable Moment of the 1960s
Jess Tyree, header manufacturer and funny car owner and driver:

"In 1964-1965, I won the Phoenix Nationals with a two-year-old 1963 A/FX Pontiac Tempest powered by a 421 Super Duty engine, defeating the factory-backed Ford Thunderbolts and Mopars. Later at the March Meet in Bakersfield, I competed with two cars, a 1962 Pontiac Catalina S/S and the Tempest 421 SD coupe, in ultra stock, which would become the A/FX class. I also ran in the Coca-Cola Cavalcade show with moderate success."

When not behind the wheel of his Mach I Mustang funny car, Gas Ronda sat behind his desk at Russ Davis Ford in Covina, California, selling high performance Ford "Cobra Jet" Mustangs. A former dance instructor, Gas suffered burns at Beeline Dragstrip in Arizona when his Mustang erupted into a ball of fire. He was never able to drive again. *Lou Hart*

The Chi-Town Hustler with Pat Minick behind the wheel captured the title, "King of the burn outs." With a John Farkonas chassis, Strange Engineering components, American Racing Engine's 426 Hemi, and Engle cams, Farkonas, Coil and Minick made an unanimous favorite among funny car fans. *Lou Hart*

Memorable Moment of the 1960s
Austin Coil, crew chief of the Chi-Town Hustler:

"With the first Chi-Town Hustler we needed exposure to get bookings to match races, so we left Chicago to go to the *Super Stock* Magazine Nationals at York, Pennsylvania. Right off the trailer, we ran an 8.17 ET, which was low ET of the meet. 'Dyno' Don Nicholson said, 'Who are these guys?'"

88

The Logghe Stamping Company built Gene Snow's "Rambunctious" Dodge Charger that had a Keith Black 426 c.i. Hemi tuned by Jake Johnston. Using a 4-inch disc Crowerglide transmission, Gene ran a 7.13 ET with a 213.77-mph speed at Rockingham. *Dale Kunesh*

The K&G Speed Association's Frantic Ford Mustang shoed by "Storm'n" Norm Weekly here for an ailing Ron Rivero at Irwindale Raceway's East vs. West Funny Car Championships. *Lou Hart*

Gary Dyer of Chicago's Mr. Norm's Super Charger drove the Ramcharger 426 Hemi, Logghe Stamping Company Dodge mini-Charger to the 1969 Coca-Cola Cavalcade of Stars Funny Car Championships. A group of selected all-star drivers would compete around the country in a series of races that would earn them points toward a championship. *Lou Hart*

Owned by Don and Roy Gay of Dickinson, Texas, "Infinity IV" was one of the most beautiful 1969 Pontiac GTOs in the country. Chassis was Logghe-built with a Keith Black 426 c.i. Hemi tuned by James Osteen, and featured a painted rainbow candy lacquer paint theme. Roy, seen at the right, handled the driving chores. *Lou Hart*

The chassis of the Blue Fox Corvette rests on the trailer showing the damaged chassis, bent tubing, missing right front wheel, and damaged "bug catcher" injector. Notice the addition of the lead weights secured by "200-mph" duct tape for handling, and to keep the front down. *Steve Delgadillo*

The "Corvette Curse" struck Norm Crowdley's Blue Fox Corvette roadster as it met its demise during a qualifying attempt at Irwindale Raceway. The 'Vette contacted the guardrail and vaulted over the railing ending up upside down and causing considerable damage to the body and chassis. Norm escaped serious injury. Mike LaPorte tuned the Chrysler Hemi-powered Corvette. *Steve Delgadillo*

Lloyd Pick throttles the Pick & Clymore A/FC injected Chevy Camaro to a 9.27 ET at 144.96 mph against Gage & Barnes' "Raunchy" 427 c.i. Hilborn injected Corvette roadster at Lions Drag Strip in Long Beach. *Bob Thompson*

93

Marv Eldridge, owner of Fiberglass Trends, manufacturer of fiberglass funny car bodies, owned and drove this candy red Corvette roadster. Powering the Corvette was a Chrysler 392 c.i. Hemi. This car participated in the Coca-Cola Cavalcade of Stars. Along with teammate Rusty Dellings in the Fiberglass Trends' AMC Javelin were strong competitors in the funny car ranks. *Steve Delgadillo*

Larry Derr in his "Glass Rat" AMC-injected, Chevy-powered A/FC funny car squares off against the Henderson Brothers' A/FC Corvette at Lions Drag Strip. *Bob Thompson*

"Mighty" Mike Van Sant piloted the 1969 "Invader" Corvette funny car here at Irwindale Raceway. Owned by Glen Sonalo and Dick Olsen, the Invader was powered by a 392 Chrysler Hemi equipped with a Howard cam, Doug Thorley headers, and Venolia pistons. The Invader set a Lions track record with an elapsed time of 7.25 ET at 202.24 mph in a final round victory over a crossed up Gordon Mineo. *Lou Hart*

"Jungle Jim" Liberman's Goodies Speed Shop-sponsored Chevy Nova featured a blown 427 Chevy motor built by Steve Kanuka. Known as drag racing's premier showman, Jungle's charisma and driving antics were his trademarks. *Dale Kunesh*

Ron O'Donnell shoed Chris "The Golden Greek" Karamesines' 1969 Plymouth Barracuda at Irwindale Raceway's East vs. West Funny Car Championships. The Kent Fuller-built chassis, with a Donavan Chrysler Hemi tuned by John Nykaza, propelled the "Chizler" to a 7.58 ET at 186.32 mph to defeat Rich Siroonian's 7.62 ET at 199 mph. *Lou Hart*

Tom Sturm's "4 Chevy Lovers" Chevy Corvair lifts the front end during a burnout at Irwindale Raceway. The Don Hardy-built Corvair had a 427 c.i. supercharged Chevy engine and was driven here by "Mighty" Mike Van Sant. *Lou Hart*

Fred Goeske prepares to use a floor jack to lift his Plymouth Dealers Association Road Runner, which was the first Road Runner-bodied funny car built. Fred participated on the Coca-Cola Cavalcade of Stars running an Exhibition Engineering chassis and a blown 392 c.i. Chrysler Hemi producing 7.60 ETs at 180 mph. *Dale Kunesh*

Roger Wolford blasts down Irwindale's 1/4-mile during a 7.68 ET at 178 mph in the Mako Shark Corvette sponsored by Jack Head Chevrolet of Alhambra, California. Don Cullinan and Jim Wetton owned and tuned the 427 c.i. blown rat motor. *Steve Delgadillo*

Mickey Thompson stands behind Johnny Wright as he shoes his white Boss 429 Mach I Mustang built by Pat Foster. Mickey's Boss 429 c.i. "Shotgun" motor broke many parts to stay competitive, and proved to be less durable than the Chrysler Hemi. *Lou Hart*

The Pisano Brothers' Exhibition Engineering-built 1969 Chevy Corvair won the 1969 Irwindale Raceway's East vs. West Funny Car Championships. Frankie, along with the "Italian Army," could do no wrong putting away the eastern competition with 7.40 ETs at 190 mph with the blown 427 c.i. Chevy rat motor. *Lou Hart*

This is what funny car pilots feared most. Tom Sturm's "Just 4 Chevy Lovers" Chevy Corvair experienced this violent blower explosion and fire that severely damaged the paint and body. *Steve Delgadillo*

Hank Clark in the "Outa' Site Too!" Chevy Camaro blasts down Irwindale's quarter mile. The Chapman Automotive Race Cars and Engines' Camaro from Chicago was powered by a 392 Chrysler Hemi tuned by Pat Johnson. *Lou Hart*

Mike Burkhart's Chevy II Nova, driven by Mart Higgenbotham, won the AHRA World Finals in Tulsa, Oklahoma. The Don Hardy-built chassis housed the nitro Chevy rat motor bored to 440 c.i. that ran a 7.52 ET at 189 mph in the final round. Shown here, Higgenbotham's Nova, tuned by Guy Tipton, carries the front wheels winning the Irwindale's 32 Funny Car Invitational Championships over Dave Beebe in the "Dodge Fever" Charger. *Lou Hart*

"Big Mike" Burkhart's Doran Chevrolet Camaro from Texas featured the fiberglass body with an opening driver's side door for the quick exit of Mike's 300-pound frame. The Camaro was powered by a supercharged 427 Chevy in a Don Hardy chassis, running a 7.44 ET at 181 mph, but losing to "The Invader" Corvette at Irwindale Raceway's 32 Funny Car Invitational. *Lou Hart*

Dick Bourgeois' "Javelin 2" was another entrant in the Coca-Cola Cavalcade of Stars carrying the AMC hopes during a 32 Funny Car Invitational Meet at Irwindale Raceway. In round two against Jess Tyree, Dick experienced blower problems at mid-track that retired him from competition. *Lou Hart*

Lee Jones pilots Malcolm Durham's "Strip Blazer VI" Chevy Camaro. The Supercar Engineering Camaro pitted against Roland Leong's "Hawaiian" lost control and vaulted over the guard railing, causing considerable damage to the Camaro. Lee walked away without serious injury thanks to Dick Fletcher's superior chassis work. *Lou Hart*

Andy Clary's TorqueMaster Converter equipped Plymouth Barracuda burns out under the lights at Irwindale Raceway. Andy, from Southern California, built the blue and white Plymouth 'Cuda, which was powered by an early Chrysler Hemi. *Lou Hart*

Ignoring the "Corvette Curse," C&O Transmissions' Gene Conway's orange Corvette roadster was a fixture around the Southern California area. The 392 c.i. Chrysler Hemi, prepped and tuned by Steve Monterelli, ran consistent 7.50 ETs with speeds over 195 mph with great success! In 1970, NHRA banned the Corvette roadster body from funny car competition. *Lou Hart*

Dee Keaton's Mercury Cougar featured a Dick Fletcher chassis, Fiberglass Trends Cougar body, and an early 392 Chrysler Hemi hooked to an Art Carr transmission. The blue Cougar was the last of the funny cars Dee owned and raced. *Steve Delgadillo*

"Fast Albert" Fontanini's Kopper-Piccone Dodge was known as the world's fastest injected funny car. The Grand Automotive mini-Charger was built by Strange Automotive and powered by a 426 c.i. nitro-injected Hemi. Unfortunately, Albert and his brother Reno lost their lives due to a highway accident when a dump truck plowed into the rear of their vehicle while they were stopped at a tollbooth. *Lou Hart*

The pits at Irwindale Raceway were standing room only, crammed with trailers, racecars, and fans. "Javelin 2" of Bourgeois & Wade readies for another Saturday night's under-the-lights action. *Steve Delgadillo*

Kumpf Motors of Denver, Colorado sponsored Kenz & Leslie's "High Country Cougar II" funny car. The "High Country Cougar II," built by Logghe, featured a 427 SOHC "Cammer" matched with a B&M Hydra-link transmission, Cyclone headers, and a Crane performance cam that powered the Wynn's-backed Cougar at Irwindale Raceway. *Lou Hart*

Ron Leslie lifts the front wheels of Kenz & Leslie's "High Country Cougar II" during a qualifying round at Irwindale Raceway. The popular Denver duo was a crowd favorite on the West Coast tour with their high wheelie launches and smoky burnouts. *Lou Hart*

"Doc" Leroy Hales in Pete Cheveron's "Wild Breed" Cougar heats the hides during Irwindale Raceway's 32 Funny Car Invitational. The ex-Dee Keaton Cougar sports a Dick Fletcher chassis, an early 392 Chrysler Hemi, an Engine Masters Torqueflite transmission, and a set of "zoomies" by Doug. *Lou Hart*

Larry Reyes piloted the "Hawaiian" of Roland Leong at Irwindale Raceway's 1969 East vs. West Funny Car Championships. The mini-Charger's Keith Black elephant powered the Logghe-built flopper to a qualifying time of 7.51 ET at 193 mph. *Lou Hart*

At the end of 1969, Jungle Jim debuted a new Logghe-built Fiberglass Ltd. Chevy Nova, switching from his traditional blue colors to this red 392 c.i. Chrysler Hemi funny car. Driver Arnie Behling turned in respectable 7.30 ETs for its first time out. *Lou Hart*

Another injected funny car was the "Smog Town Hustler" shown here at Fontana's Drag City. Many of the earlier supercharged nitro funny cars return to competition as injected funny cars turning 9.30 ETs at 165 mph. *Bob Thompson*

Gas Ronda's Ed Pink-powered 427 SOHC Mach I carries the front wheels prior to breaking the driveline during Irwindale Raceway's 32 Funny Car Invitational Championships. Skip Burroughs tuned the popular Mustang to win the 1969 OCIR Manufacturers Meet and defeat Pat Minick in the "Chi-Town Hustler" in the final round. *Steve Delgadillo*

Memorable Moment of the 1960s
Bill Crites, Photographer:

"Being with so many people, we were like family. With the likes of Dale Armstrong, Ray Alley, McEwen, Shirley, Jungle Jim, we experienced growing up together and at times, we lost members of our family too, which was really hard on all of us."

Don Hampton in the Beach City Chevrolet Corvette takes on Larry Reyes in Roland Leong's "Hawaiian" at a packed house at Irwindale Raceway. Donnie took out Reyes on a tremendous holeshot during eliminations with a 7.58 ET at 193 mph. *Steve Delgadillo*

Smokey Joe Lee from San Diego was the West Coast's answer to the "Chi-Town Hustler's" awesome burnouts! The former top fuel pilot always put the fans on their feet with his awesome driving abilities. *Lou Hart*

Charlie Allen debuted the first-ever 1970 Dodge Challenger funny car built by M&S Welding with Jeff Crowther tuning the Keith Black 426 Hemi running a dialed-in 7.56 ET at 189 mph. *Lou Hart*

123

Danny Ongais earned "Drag News Driver of the Year" for 1969. Danny set numerous records for ETs, and was credited with running a controversial 6.95 ET at Kansas City Raceway, and winning several NHRA National events throughout the country. *Dale Kunesh*

Randy Walls was a die-hard Chevy owner and driver who made a living racing and building his own cars. Randy never switched to the Chrysler Hemi and he utilized his knowledge of the Chevy rat motor, seldom breaking or damaging parts. On one occasion, Randy used a Hertz rental car one weekend to mold his own Nova bodies. This process entailed filling in the seams of the trunk, doors and hood with green clay, removing all handles, wipers and trim, and covering the Nova with cellophane. He then laid down strips of soaked material into hardening agents and left them to dry. The hardest part was making sure that all the green clay was removed from the door jams using a lot of car wax and elbow grease before returning the car to Hertz. *Photo courtesy of Randy Walls' scrapbook*

Rich Siroonian lifts the front wheels of the candy apple red Plymouth Barracuda of "Big John" Mazmanian. The 392 c.i. Hemi built by Keith Black was prepped and tuned by Doug Cook and was wrapped in an Exhibition Engineering chassis. "Big John," a giant of the gasser wars, along with the "Armanian Army," always provided Don Schumacher and Mickey Thompson with many long nights at the track. *Lou Hart*

Memorable Moment of the 1960s
Rich Siroonian:

"Winning the 1968 Orange County International Raceway Sixty-Four Funny Car Manufacturers Meet in the final round against Don Schumacher and John Hogan."

AMERICAN CULTURE

Coca-Cola: A History in Photographs 1930-1969 ISBN 1-882256-46-8
Coca-Cola: Its Vehicles in Photographs 1930-1969 ISBN 1-882256-47-6
Phillips 66 1945-1954 Photo Archive ISBN 1-882256-42-5

AUTOMOTIVE

AMX Photo Archive: From Concept to Reality ISBN 1-58388-062-3
Auburn Automobiles 1900-1936 Photo Archive ISBN 1-58388-093-3
Camaro 1967-2000 Photo Archive ISBN 1-58388-032-1
Checker Cab Co. Photo History ISBN 1-58388-100-X
Chevrolet Station Wagons 1946-1966 Photo Archive ISBN 1-58388-069-0
Classic American Limousines 1955-2000 Photo Archive ISBN 1-58388-041-0
Corvair by Chevrolet Experimental & Production Cars 1957-1969, Ludvigsen Library Series ISBN 1-58388-058-5
Corvette The Exotic Experimental Cars, Ludvigsen Library Series ISBN 1-58388-017-8
Corvette Prototypes & Show Cars Photo Album ISBN 1-882256-77-8
Early Ford V-8s 1932-1942 Photo Album ISBN 1-882256-97-2
Ferrari- The Factory Maranello's Secrets 1950-1975, Ludvigsen Library Series ISBN 1-58388-085-2
Ford Postwar Flatheads 1946-1953 Photo Archive ISBN 1-58388-080-1
Ford Station Wagons 1929-1991 Photo History ISBN 1-58388-103-4
Imperial 1955-1963 Photo Archive ISBN 1-882256-22-0
Imperial 1964-1968 Photo Archive ISBN 1-882256-23-9
Javelin Photo Archive: From Concept to Reality ISBN 1-58388-071-2
Lincoln Motor Cars 1920-1942 Photo Archive ISBN 1-882256-57-3
Lincoln Motor Cars 1946-1960 Photo Archive ISBN 1-882256-58-1
Nash 1936-1957 Photo Archive ISBN 1-58388-086-0
Packard Motor Cars 1935-1942 Photo Archive ISBN 1-882256-44-1
Packard Motor Cars 1946-1958 Photo Archive ISBN 1-882256-45-X
Pontiac Dream Cars, Show Cars & Prototypes 1928-1998 Photo Album ISBN 1-882256-93-X
Pontiac Firebird Trans-Am 1969-1999 Photo Album ISBN 1-882256-95-6
Pontiac Firebird 1967-2000 Photo History ISBN 1-58388-028-3
Rambler 1950-1969 Photo Archive ISBN 1-58388-078-X
Stretch Limousines 1928-2001 Photo Archive ISBN 1-58388-070-4
Studebaker 1933-1942 Photo Archive ISBN 1-882256-24-7
Studebaker Hawk 1956-1964 Photo Archive ISBN 1-58388-094-1
Studebaker Lark 1959-1966 Photo Archive ISBN 1-58388-107-7
Ultimate Corvette Trivia Challenge ISBN 1-58388-035-6

BUSES

Buses of ACF Photo Archive ISBN 1-58388-101-8
Buses of Motor Coach Industries 1932-2000 Photo Archive ISBN 1-58388-039-9
Fageol & Twin Coach Buses 1922-1956 Photo Archive ISBN 1-58388-075-5
Flxible Intercity Buses 1924-1970 Photo Archive ISBN 1-58388-108-5
Flxible Transit Buses 1953-1995 Photo Archive ISBN 1-58388-053-4
GM Intercity Coaches 1944-1980 Photo Archive ISBN 1-58388-099-2
Greyhound Buses 1914-2000 Photo Archive ISBN 1-58388-027-5
*Mack® Buses 1900-1960 Photo Archive** ISBN 1-58388-020-8
Prevost Buses 1924-2002 Photo Archive ISBN 1-58388-083-6
Trailways Buses 1936-2001 Photo Archive ISBN 1-58388-029-1
Trolley Buses 1913-2001 Photo Archive ISBN 1-58388-057-7
Yellow Coach Buses 1923-1943 Photo Archive ISBN 1-58388-054-2

EMERGENCY VEHICLES

The American Ambulance 1900-2002: An Illustrated History ISBN 1-58388-081-X
American Funeral Vehicles 1883-2003 Illustrated History ISBN 1-58388-104-2
American LaFrance 700 Series 1945-1952 Photo Archive ISBN 1-882256-90-5
American LaFrance 700 Series 1945-1952 Photo Archive Volume 2 ISBN 1-58388-025-9
American LaFrance 700 & 800 Series 1953-1958 Photo Archive ISBN 1-882256-91-3
American LaFrance 900 Series 1958-1964 Photo Archive ISBN 1-58388-002-X
Classic Seagrave 1935-1951 Photo Archive ISBN 1-58388-034-8
Crown Firecoach 1951-1985 Photo Archive ISBN 1-58388-047-X
Fire Chief Cars 1900-1997 Photo Album ISBN 1-882256-87-5
Hahn Fire Apparatus 1923-1990 Photo Archive ISBN 1-58388-077-1
Heavy Rescue Trucks 1931-2000 Photo Gallery ISBN 1-58388-045-3
Imperial Fire Apparatus 1969-1976 Photo Archive ISBN 1-58388-091-7
Industrial and Private Fire Apparatus 1925-2001 Photo Archive ISBN 1-58388-049-6
Los Angeles City Fire Apparatus 1953-1999 Photo Archive ISBN 1-58388-012-7
*Mack Model C Fire Trucks 1957-1967 Photo Archive** ISBN 1-58388-014-3
*Mack Model L Fire Trucks 1940-1954 Photo Archive** ISBN 1-882256-86-7
Maxim Fire Apparatus 1914-1989 Photo Archive ISBN 1-58388-050-X
Navy & Marine Corps Fire Apparatus 1836 -2000 Photo Gallery ISBN 1-58388-031-3
Pierre Thibault Ltd. Fire Apparatus 1918-1990 Photo Archive ISBN 1-58388-074-7
Pirsch Fire Apparatus 1890-1991 Photo Archive ISBN 1-58388-082-8
Police Cars: Restoring, Collecting & Showing America's Finest Sedans ISBN 1-58388-046-1
Saulsbury Fire Rescue Apparatus 1956-2003 Photo Archive ISBN 1-58388-106-9
Seagrave 70th Anniversary Series Photo Archive ISBN 1-58388-001-1
TASC Fire Apparatus 1946-1985 Photo Archive ISBN 1-58388-065-8
Volunteer & Rural Fire Apparatus Photo Gallery ISBN 1-58388-005-4
W.S. Darley & Co. Fire Apparatus 1908-2000 Photo Archive ISBN 1-58388-061-5
Ward LaFrance Fire Trucks 1918-1978 Photo Archive ISBN 1-58388-013-5
Wildland Fire Apparatus 1940-2001 Photo Gallery ISBN 1-58388-056-9
Young Fire Equipment 1932-1991 Photo Archive ISBN 1-58388-015-1

RACING

Chaparral Can-Am Racing Cars from Texas, Ludvigsen Library Series ISBN 1-58388-066-6
Cunningham Sports Cars, Ludvigsen Library Series ISBN 1-58388-109-3
Drag Racing Funny Cars of the 1960s Photo Archive ISBN 1-58388-097-6
Drag Racing Funny Cars of the 1970s Photo Archive ISBN 1-58388-068-2
El Mirage Impressions: Dry Lakes Land Speed Racing ISBN 1-58388-059-3
GT40 Photo Archive ISBN 1-882256-64-6
Indy Cars of the 1950s, Ludvigsen Library Series ISBN 1-58388-018-6
Indy Cars of the 1960s, Ludvigsen Library Series ISBN 1-58388-052-6
Indy Cars of the 1970s, Ludvigsen Library Series ISBN 1-58388-098-4
Indianapolis Racing Cars of Frank Kurtis 1941-1963 Photo Archive ISBN 1-58388-026-7
Juan Manuel Fangio World Champion Driver Series Photo Album ISBN 1-58388-008-9

More Great Titles From Iconografix

All Iconografix books are available from direct mail specialty book dealers and bookstores worldwide, or can be ordered from the publisher. For book trade and distribution information or to add your name to our mailing list and receive a **FREE CATALOG** contact:

Iconografix,
PO Box 446, Dept BK
Hudson, WI, 54016

Telephone: (715) 381-9755,
(800) 289-3504 (USA),
Fax: (715) 381-9756

*This product is sold under license from Mack Trucks, Inc. Mack is a registered Trademark of Mack Trucks, Inc. All rights reserved.

Lost Race Tracks Treasures of Automobile Racing ISBN 1-58388-084-4
Mario Andretti World Champion Driver Series Photo Album ISBN 1-58388-009-7
Mercedes-Benz 300SL Racing Cars 1952-1953, Ludvigsen Library Series ISBN 1-58388-067-4
Novi V-8 Indy Cars 1941-1965, Ludvigsen Library Series ISBN 1-58388-037-2
Porsche Spyders Type 550 1953-1956, Ludvigsen Library Series ISBN 1-58388-092-5
Sebring 12-Hour Race 1970 Photo Archive ISBN 1-882256-20-4
Vanderbilt Cup Race 1936 & 1937 Photo Archive ISBN 1-882256-66-2

RAILWAYS

Chicago, St. Paul, Minneapolis & Omaha Railway 1880-1940 Photo Archive ISBN 1-882256-67-0
Chicago & North Western Railway 1975-1995 Photo Archive ISBN 1-882256-76-X
Great Northern Railway 1945-1970 Volume 2 Photo Archive ISBN 1-882256-79-4
Great Northern Railway Ore Docks of Lake Superior Photo Archive ISBN 1-58388-073-9
Illinois Central Railroad 1854-1960 Photo Archive ISBN 1-58388-063-1
Milwaukee Road 1850-1960 Photo Archive ISBN 1-882256-61-1
Milwaukee Road Depots 1856-1954 Photo Archive ISBN 1-58388-040-2
Show Trains of the 20th Century ISBN 1-58388-030-5
Soo Line 1975-1992 Photo Archive ISBN 1-882256-68-9
Steam Locomotives of the B&O Railroad Photo Archive ISBN 1-58388-095-X
Streamliners to the Twin Cities Photo Archive 400, Twin Zephyrs & Hiawatha Trains ISBN 1-58388-096-8
Trains of the Twin Ports Photo Archive, Duluth-Superior in the 1950s ISBN 1-58388-003-8
Trains of the Circus 1872-1956 ISBN 1-58388-024-0
Trains of the Upper Midwest Photo Archive Steam & Diesel in the 1950s & 1960s ISBN 1-58388-036-4
Wisconsin Central Limited 1987-1996 Photo Archive ISBN 1-882256-75-1
Wisconsin Central Railway 1871-1909 Photo Archive ISBN 1-882256-78-6

RECREATIONAL VEHICLES

Ski-Doo Racing Sleds 1960-2003 Photo Archive ISBN 1-58388-105-0

TRUCKS

Autocar Trucks 1950-1987 Photo Archive ISBN 1-58388-072-0
Beverage Trucks 1910-1975 Photo Archive ISBN 1-882256-60-3
*Brockway Trucks 1948-1961 Photo Archive** ISBN 1-882256-55-7
Chevrolet El Camino Photo History Incl. GMC Sprint & Caballero ISBN 1-58388-044-5
Circus and Carnival Trucks 1923-2000 Photo Archive ISBN 1-58388-048-8
Dodge B-Series Trucks Restorer's & Collector's Reference Guide and History ISBN 1-58388-087-9
Dodge Pickups 1939-1978 Photo Album ISBN 1-882256-82-4
Dodge Power Wagons 1940-1980 Photo Archive ISBN 1-882256-89-1
Dodge Power Wagon Photo History ISBN 1-58388-019-4
Dodge Ram Trucks 1994-2001 Photo History ISBN 1-58388-051-8
Dodge Trucks 1929-1947 Photo Archive ISBN 1-882256-36-0
Dodge Trucks 1948-1960 Photo Archive ISBN 1-882256-37-9
Ford 4x4s 1935-1990 Photo History ISBN 1-58388-079-8
Ford Heavy-Duty Trucks 1948-1998 Photo History ISBN 1-58388-043-7
Freightliner Trucks 1937-1981 Photo Archive ISBN 1-58388-090-9
Jeep 1941-2000 Photo Archive ISBN 1-58388-021-6
Jeep Prototypes & Concept Vehicles Photo Archive ISBN 1-58388-033-X
*Mack Model AB Photo Archive** ISBN 1-882256-18-2
*Mack AP Super-Duty Trucks 1926-1938 Photo Archive** ISBN 1-882256-54-9
*Mack Model B 1953-1966 Volume 2 Photo Archive** ISBN 1-882256-34-4
*Mack EB-EC-ED-EE-EF-EG-DE 1936-1951 Photo Archive** ISBN 1-882256-29-8
*Mack EH-EJ-EM-EQ-ER-ES 1936-1950 Photo Archive** ISBN 1-882256-39-5
*Mack FC-FCSW-NW 1936-1947 Photo Archive** ISBN 1-882256-28-X
*Mack FG-FH-FJ-FK-FN-FP-FT-FW 1937-1950 Photo Archive** ISBN 1-882256-35-2
*Mack LF-LH-LJ-LM-LT 1940-1956 Photo Archive** ISBN 1-882256-38-7
*Mack Trucks Photo Gallery** ISBN 1-882256-88-3
New Car Carriers 1910-1998 Photo Album ISBN 1-882256-98-0
Plymouth Commercial Vehicles Photo Archive ISBN 1-58388-004-6
Refuse Trucks Photo Archive ISBN 1-58388-042-9
RVs & Campers 1900-2000: An Illustrated History ISBN 1-58388-064-X
Studebaker Trucks 1927-1940 Photo Archive ISBN 1-882256-40-9
White Trucks 1900-1937 Photo Archive ISBN 1-882256-80-8

TRACTORS & CONSTRUCTION EQUIPMENT

Case Tractors 1912-1959 Photo Archive ISBN 1-882256-32-8
Caterpillar Photo Gallery ISBN 1-882256-70-0
Caterpillar Pocket Guide The Track-Type Tractors 1925-1957 ISBN 1-58388-022-4
Caterpillar D-2 & R-2 Photo Archive ISBN 1-882256-99-9
Caterpillar D-8 1933-1974 Photo Archive Incl. Diesel 75 & RD-8 ISBN 1-882256-96-4
Caterpillar Military Tractors Volume 1 Photo Archive ISBN 1-882256-16-6
Caterpillar Military Tractors Volume 2 Photo Archive ISBN 1-882256-17-4
Caterpillar Sixty Photo Archive ISBN 1-882256-05-0
Caterpillar Ten Photo Archive Incl. 7c Fifteen & High Fifteen ISBN 1-58388-011-9
Caterpillar Thirty Photo Archive 2ND Ed. Incl. Best Thirty, 6G Thirty & R-4 ISBN 1-58388-006-2
Circus & Carnival Tractors 1930-2001 Photo Archive ISBN 1-58388-076-3
Cletrac and Oliver Crawlers Photo Archive ISBN 1-882256-43-3
Classic American Steamrollers 1871-1935 Photo Archive ISBN 1-58388-038-0
Farmall Cub Photo Archive ISBN 1-882256-71-9
Farmall F-Series Photo Archive ISBN 1-882256-02-6
Farmall Model H Photo Archive ISBN 1-882256-03-4
Farmall Model M Photo Archive ISBN 1-882256-15-8
Farmall Regular Photo Archive ISBN 1-882256-14-X
Farmall Super Series Photo Archive ISBN 1-882256-49-2
Fordson 1917-1928 Photo Archive ISBN 1-882256-33-6
Hart-Parr Photo Archive ISBN 1-882256-08-5
Holt Tractors Photo Archive ISBN 1-882256-10-7
International TracTracTor Photo Archive ISBN 1-882256-48-4
John Deere Model A Photo Archive ISBN 1-882256-12-3
John Deere Model D Photo Archive ISBN 1-882256-00-X
Marion Construction Machinery 1884-1975 Photo Archive ISBN 1-58388-060-7
Marion Mining & Dredging Machines Photo Archive ISBN 1-58388-088-7
Oliver Tractors Photo Archive ISBN 1-882256-09-3
Russell Graders Photo Archive ISBN 1-882256-11-5
Twin City Tractor Photo Archive ISBN 1-882256-06-9

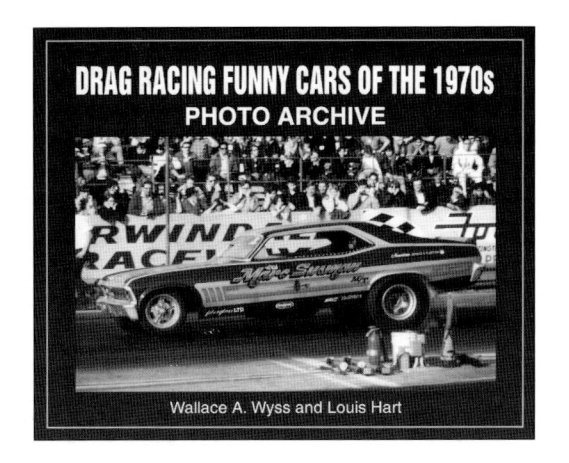

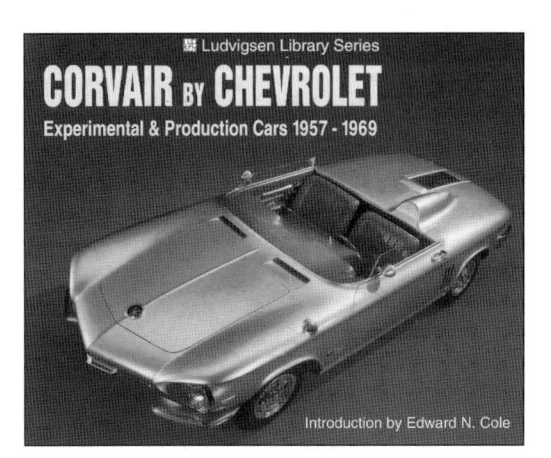

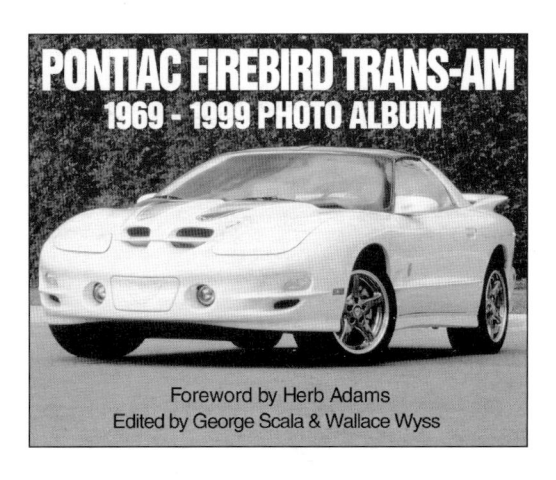

More great books from
Iconografix

Drag Racing Funny Cars of the 1970s Photo Archive
ISBN 1-58388-068-2

Early Ford V-8s 1932-1942 Photo Album
ISBN 1-882256-97-2

Corvair by Chevrolet: Experimental & Production Cars 1957-1969
ISBN 1-58388-058-5

AMX Photo Archive: From Concept to Reality
ISBN 1-58388-062-3

Pontiac Firebird Trans-Am 1969-1999 Photo Album
ISBN 1-882256-95-6

Pontiac Firebird 1967-2000 Photo History
ISBN 1-58388-028-3

Javelin Photo Archive: From Concept to Reality
ISBN 1-58388-071-2

Iconografix, Inc.
P.O. Box 446, Dept BK,
Hudson, WI 54016
For a **free catalog** call**:** 1-800-289-3504

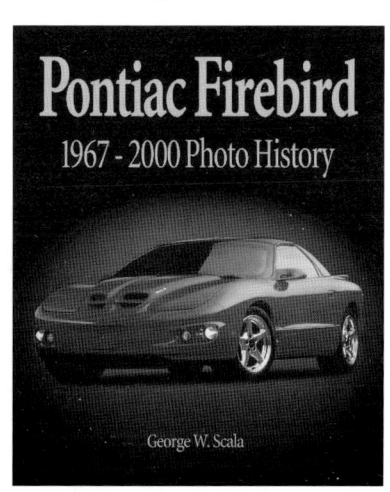

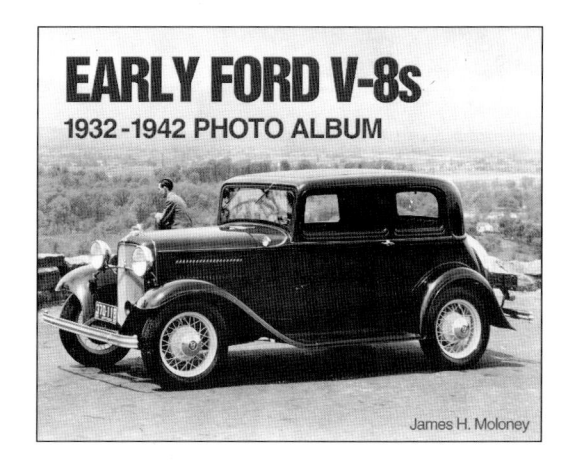

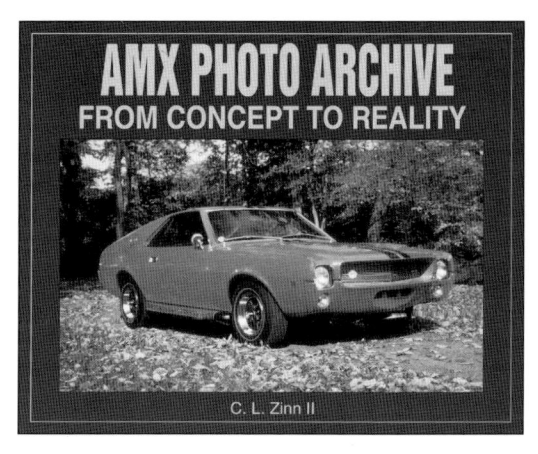

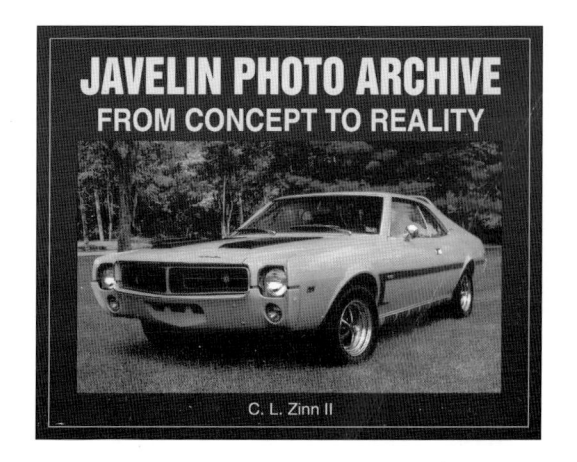